I0887577

SPOTLIGHT ON NATURE

KOMODO DRAGON

PAMELA DELL

CREATIVE EDUCATION · CREATIVE PAPERBACKS

Published by Creative Education and Creative Paperbacks
P.O. Box 227, Mankato, Minnesota 56002
Creative Education and Creative Paperbacks
are imprints of The Creative Company
www.thecreativecompany.us

Design and production by Blue Design, Inc.
Art direction by Wyeth Morgan
Edited by Grace Beltowski

Photographs by Dreamstime/Liliya Butenko, 8, 10, 14, 16, 20, 22, Md Saidur Rahman, 3, 6, 29, Pebat, 11, Sergey Uryadnikov, 10, Steve Wilson, 21, Zune Shing Lim, 21; Getty Images/FEBRUARY, 28, Fox Photos, 27, Jakob Polacsek, 23, Maria Swärd, 4–5, Marko Konig, 15, Michael Dunning, 14, 18, Michele Westmorland, 12, Suryani Edy / 500px, 29, Tony Shi Photography, 17, Viv Vivekananda / 500px, 6; iStock/9; Shutterstock/kkaplin, 16; Unsplash/Dennis Schmidt, cover, 1, Guillaume Marques, 24; Wikimedia Commons/Christoph Moning, 29, Mats Stafseng Einarsen, 29

Library of Congress Cataloging-in-Publication Data
Names: Dell, Pamela, author.
Title: Komodo dragon / Pamela Dell.
Description: Mankato, Minnesota : Creative Education / Creative Paperbacks, [2026] | Series: Spotlight on nature | Includes bibliographical references and index. | Audience: Ages 10-13 | Audience: Grades 4-6 | Summary: "Saunter into the Komodo dragon's world with this nature title for middle-grade wildlife lovers. Informational text pairs with a narrative about a single monitor lizard family to spotlight the wild animal's life cycle, supported by infographics and a timeline of developmental milestones"— Provided by publisher.
Identifiers: LCCN 2024048401 (print) | LCCN 2024048402 (ebook) | ISBN 9798889896241 (library binding) | ISBN 9781682777909 (paperback) | ISBN 9798889897040 (ebook)
Classification: LCC QL666.L29 D45 2026 (print) | LCC QL666.L29 (ebook) | DDC 597.95/968—dc23/eng/20250102
LC record available at https://lccn.loc.gov/2024048401
LC ebook record available at https://lccn.loc.gov/2024048402

Printed in India

CONTENTS

MEET THE FAMILY

KOMODO DRAGONS of Indonesia

A rare treasure exists on a handful of volcanic islands in Southeast Asia. These islands are Flores, Komodo, Rinca, Gili Montang, and Gili Desami. The last four are part of Indonesia's Komodo National Park. But that's not their claim to fame. The island habitat is a world of tropical forests, steep hills, and dry, open grasslands. Large mammals, such as wild boar, water buffalo, and Timor deer, roam the islands. Many **species** of birds and snakes, including the deadly cobra, live here, too. But the most notable wildlife of all is the Komodo dragon. Found nowhere else on Earth in the wild, these massive reptiles are what make the islands unique.

It's late August, and a female Komodo dragon is digging several deep holes in the ground. Into one of them, she lays about 30 eggs. After nearly nine months, in April or May, her young are ready to hatch.

CLOSE-UP

Vision

The Komodo dragon has extremely sharp eye-sight during the day. It can see as far away as the length of 3 football fields, or 980 feet (300 meters) But it has trouble identifying objects that aren't moving. Scientists also believe dragons have poor night vision.

CHAPTER ONE

LIFE BEGINS

Reptiles have a big place in the world. They include more than 11,000 different species. But the Komodo dragon rules. It belongs to a group of about 50 venomous species known as monitor lizards. And of all the world's reptiles, none are larger or heavier than the Komodo dragon.

Fully grown, males typically measure about 8 feet (2.4 m) long. They weigh as much as 200 pounds (90.7 kilograms). Scientists have even measured some as big as 10 feet (3 m) long and 300 pounds (136 kg) in weight. Female Komodo dragons are usually slightly smaller than males.

When morning comes, the Komodo dragon crawls out of its cave, ready for some sun. Its island habitat lies only a few hundred miles south of the Equator, so it's hot. This is a good thing. Like all reptiles, dragons are **ectothermic**. They need outside sources of heat to warm their bodies and stay alive. So sun baths are a daily necessity. After soaking up the rays, they are energized. If they are hungry enough, they may go hunting.

KOMODO DRAGON MILESTONES

DAY 1

- Hatches from egg
- Immediately retreats up trees
- Weight: 3.5 ounces (100 grams)
- Length: 15 inches (38.1 centimeters)
- Brightly colored with yellow, green, or reddish spots and stripes on a dark body

Komodo dragons are fierce, frightening **apex predators**. Except during mating season, they don't like company. They are **carnivorous**. They hunt solo, hiding in tall grasses to **ambush** their unsuspecting prey. They target animals even bigger than themselves, such as water buffalo, wild pigs, and deer. But dragons will eat meat in almost any form. This includes carrion, or dead animal carcasses, and fish that wash to shore. Although it's rare, they have sometimes been known to attack or even kill human beings. Dragons are also cannibals. They have no problem eating each other, especially their own babies.

CLOSE-UP

Ears

Komodo dragons don't have visible ears. Their hearing comes through the holes on the sides of their head. The dragon's sense of hearing isn't that sharp, but its ears are important to help the animal keep its balance.

Mother dragons usually lay their eggs in late August or September. For the first few months, a female will watchfully guard her nest. But

FEATURED FAMILY

Welcome to the World

Baby Komodo dragons have their work cut out for them. They begin life inside a tough, leathery shell about the size of a grapefruit. Escaping is hard and tiring. A small, horny knob on its snout, called an egg tooth, helps the **hatchling** break free. Then it needs a long rest before digging out of the nest. Hatchlings are surprisingly small but fully developed. Only their skin looks different than that of a full-grown adult. The babies have dark bodies with brightly colored stripes and spots. These colors are usually yellow, green, or sometimes reddish hues.

by December she is gone. Four or five months later, the eggs hatch. The hatchlings emerge during the wet season, so food is easy to find. But their mother has abandoned them long before. They've got no one to show them the ropes. These little creatures **instinctively** head for the trees soon after hatching. Now it's up to them to figure out how to stay alive.

9 MONTHS

- Grown to about 2 pounds (0.9 kg) and 18 inches (45.7 cm)
- Still lives mostly in trees
- Siblings stay together
- Eats mainly insects and small lizards such as geckos

CLOSE-UP

Skull and jaw

The Komodo dragon's unique, lightweight skull differs from those of other large predators. Because of the skull's flattened, side-to-side shape, the dragon's bite is weaker but still forceful. Its jaws are still excellent at ripping flesh and bringing down prey larger than itself.

FEATURED FAMILY

First Meal

Komodo dragons get no baby food brought by their mother. On their own, hatchlings soon flee the nest. They scramble up trees, for both safety and food. First meals include grasshoppers, beetles, and other insects crawling the tree branches. Later, when they have grown a bit, young dragons add geckos and other small lizards to their diet. Birds' eggs are a tasty treat, too. These guys also stick to the treetops for safety's sake. Adult dragons are too heavy to climb. If they could, even their own mothers might catch and eat their young.

BABY KOMODO DRAGONS are on their own from the moment they escape their shell.

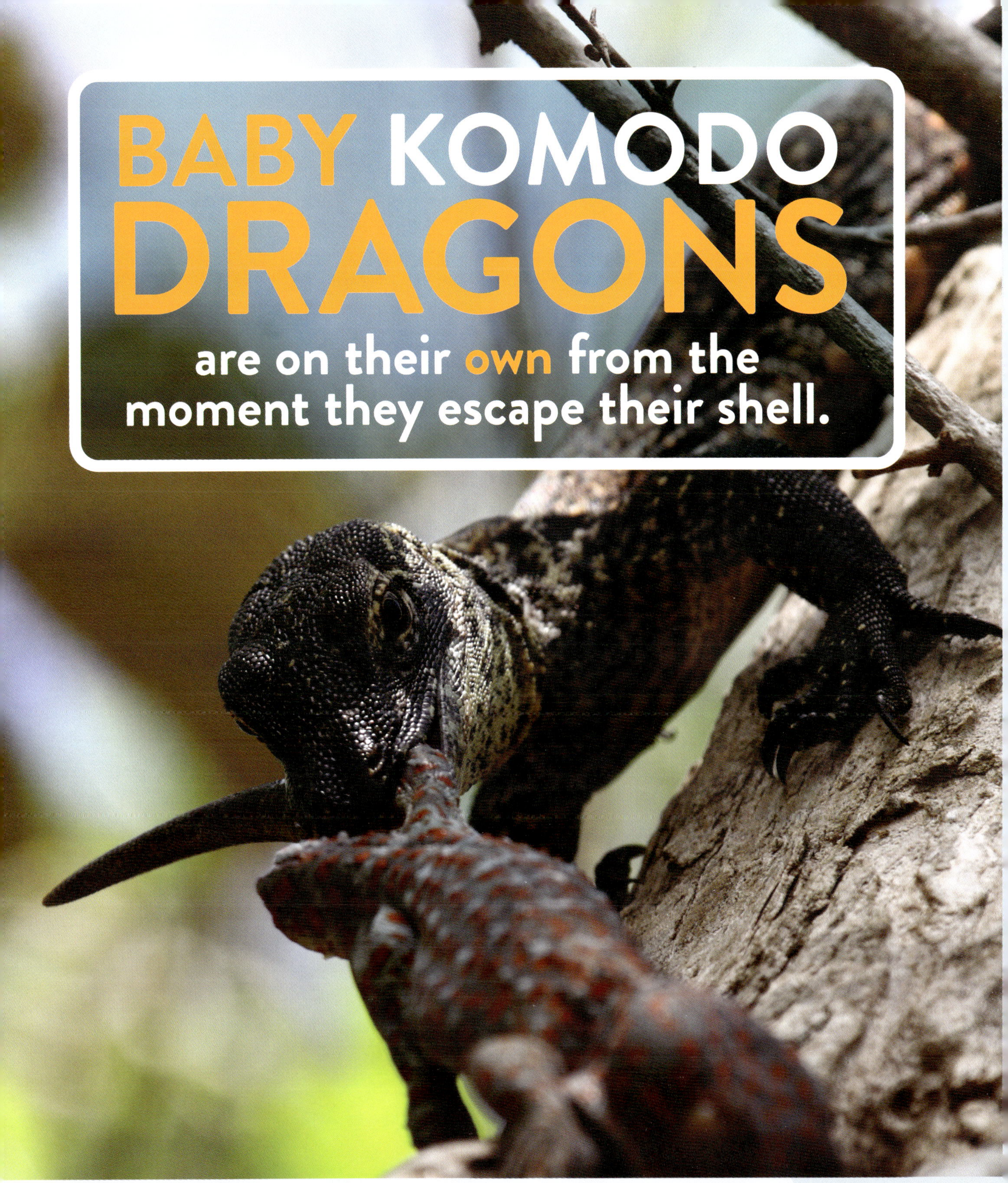

1 YEAR

- Makes rare trips to the ground for more food
- Diet expands to include snakes, chicken eggs, and small ground mammals such as rats

CLOSE-UP

Forked tongue

The Komodo dragon's acute sense of smell comes mostly from its long, forked tongue. The tongue and a special organ on the roof of the dragon's mouth together pick up scent particles in the air. Dragons can even sniff out carrion from several miles away.

CHAPTER TWO

EARLY ADVENTURES

It's time to take a risk! By about two years old, Komodo dragons have left babyhood behind. They begin to venture out of the trees. Insects no longer provide enough food. They need real meat, such as rodents and other small mammals. Now that they are bigger, their own kind are the only predators they need to fear.

Fortunately, even young Komodo dragons have tools to help them out. Their long, forked tongues give them information about odors in the air, even from long distances. That means they are keenly tuned in to the smells around them. The scent of other dragons tells them to be cautious. That tongue also alerts them to where they can find prey when hunger pangs strike.

With its bowed legs, the Komodo dragon's body sways slightly from side to side as it walks. Its powerful tail moves back and forth to help the animal stay balanced. All this gives the dragon a bulky and awkward-looking

2 YEARS

- Begins experimenting with life on the ground
- Siblings separate, becoming more territorial

4 YEARS

- No longer small enough to climb trees
- Begins living fulltime on the ground

CLOSE-UP

Teeth

The Komodo dragon's 60 razor-sharp teeth are deadly weapons. Some of these teeth may measure as long as 1 inch (2.5 cm). Dragons frequently lose teeth because of their vicious hunting and fighting behavior. But these are constantly replaced throughout the reptile's lifetime.

FEATURED FAMILY

Leaving the Trees

The bigger Komodo dragons grow, the more independent they become. The trees kept them safe as youngsters. Sharing life with their siblings wasn't a problem. But now they are getting big. They need more food. They need more room. They want to establish their own territory. The only way to accomplish all this is by living on the ground. No one has taught them anything up until this point. They've learned it all on their own. This will have to continue down below. It's time to abandon life in the trees.

appearance. But it can move fast when necessary. Komodo dragons have clocked speeds of up to 13 miles (21 kilometers) an hour.

Speed is a good thing when pursuing a meal. And hunting comes naturally. But young Komodo dragons need other tactics to avoid becoming a dragon's meal themselves. Luckily, they have a tricky—and smelly—way to keep the attention off themselves. To ward off bigger or older dragons, the young ones will roll around in fecal matter, or poop. The old guys will always avoid that nasty smell.

5 YEARS

- Weight: 55 pounds (25 kg)
- Length: 6.5 feet (2 m)

CLOSE-UP

Venom

As a Komodo dragon rips away its victim's flesh, a deadly poison, or venom, squirts from between its teeth. The venom works quickly. Blood loss causes the prey's blood pressure to drop. Then it goes into shock, too weak to get away.

FEATURED FAMILY

Give It a Try

Trying life on the ground is unavoidable. But at mealtime, there's something young Komodo dragons do *not* want to try. That's getting to the table first. Mating is not the only reason dragons may come together. They often gather in groups when there's a big kill to share. In these situations, the group dynamic is all about size. The biggest, most dominant dragons go first, ripping out huge chunks of their victim's flesh. Younger, smaller dragons must wait their turn. If they don't, they may become part of the meal.

Their bowed legs make them look slow and clunky, but Komodo **DRAGONS** can **out-run** most humans.

7 YEARS

- Females reach their full size
- Males may continue to grow over many more years

CLOSE-UP

Claws

Sharp, curved claws adorn each of the Komodo dragon's four feet. These claws aren't just useful as weapons in seizing prey. They also come in handy for digging nests. And young dragons need them to escape up into trees.

CHAPTER THREE

LIFE LESSONS

It is almost impossible to tell the difference physically between a male Komodo dragon and a female. But from what they do know about this, scientists are discovering a sad fact. Male dragons seem to live much longer than females. In the wild, a male's lifespan might be as much as 50 or 60 years. But female dragons seem to live only about 32 years. Researchers think this is probably due to all the "housekeeping" the female does. It takes much energy to grow and produce eggs. A month or more of nest building every year also takes its toll. Further energy is used up in the months she spends guarding her nest.

Females reach sexual maturity at about eight or nine years old. This is when they first try nest building. Males may become mature around the same time. But researchers don't really know for sure. Younger males are, of course, smaller and weaker than older males.

8–9 YEARS

- Mates for first time

Male dragons often fight ferociously over females. So even if the younger ones are ready to mate, they hold back. They know these are battles they cannot win.

Young dragons also learn to be cautious at group meals. These events are gory and gross. Dragons cannot chew. They swallow their victim's flesh in whole chunks. They eat almost every part of their prey. This includes horns, hooves, skin, bones, and hair. Later, they will vomit up these indigestible parts. The victim's stomach and intestines are about the only thing dragons won't eat.

Often, vicious fighting breaks out among equal-sized dragons competing to eat first. The loser may not just lose dinner. If they don't back off fast enough, they could lose their life. In all this violence, the practice of covering themselves in poop comes especially in handy for

FEATURED FAMILY

This Is How Its Done

Young Komodo dragons have a few other ways to avoid their hungry elders. Because dragons don't eat intestines, the organ acts as a safety zone. The adolescents will hide among the entrails. They rest quietly in the slime, remaining unseen while the others feed. Another useful tactic makes them more noticeable. To keep the elders calm, young dragons perform exaggerated movements as they walk around the feeding circle. Their tails stick straight out behind them. Their bodies jerk roughly from side to side as they move. This shows they mean no harm.

CLOSE-UP

Tail

The Komodo dragon's thick, powerful tail stores fat reserves. It can also bring down an enemy in one swipe. The tail helps the animal stand up in combat and stay balanced when running. It also serves as a paddle during a swim.

32 YEARS

Average end of life for females in the wild

the younger ones. It helps them go unnoticed in the crowd. Because of their smell, bigger dragons won't go near them. If the youngsters remain alive, they'll eat later.

In this and everything else, these young reptiles are entirely self-taught. The knowledge of how to fight, hunt prey, and stay safe from bigger dragons comes naturally. With any luck, these skills will keep a young Komodo dragon alive for a long time.

CLOSE-UP

Scales

Chain mail is a type of armor that protected the knights of old in battle. A Komodo dragon's skin is made of scales full of tiny bones. These scales give the skin its protective quality, just like chain mail did for the knights.

FEATURED FAMILY

Practice Makes Perfect

Young Komodo dragons have a built-in hunting instinct. They hide in the grass. Their long, forked tongues dart in and out, detecting the scent of prey. If the left fork gets more sensory input, it means the prey is somewhere to the left. Same with the right fork. When a wild boar or other prey approaches, these young predators move stealthily—then they lunge! The unsuspecting prey drops. A dragon's deadly claws and savage, venomous bite spell death. If the victim escapes, no problem. Komodo dragons will track the animal by scent while it's dying from poison and blood loss.

In their brutal battles

FOR MATES AND MEALS,

male Komodo dragons stand on their back legs and use their tails for support.

60 YEARS

- Average end of life for males in the wild

CHAPTER FOUR

KOMODO COMEBACK

Outside of zoos, a few Indonesian islands are Komodo dragons' only home. But they didn't always live there. Recent studies have revealed something surprising. These giant lizards probably started out in Australia millions of years ago. Fossil records back this up. Then, about 900,000 years ago, these ancestors of the modern-day dragon disappeared from Australia. Somehow they landed in Indonesia.

Science has also determined that millions of years ago the Komodo dragon was just one of several truly gigantic reptile species. But today, the dragon is the last giant species surviving. It is the only one that has not gone **extinct**.

Conservationists around the globe are working to keep it that way. But Komodo dragons face many threats. People are a major danger. The dragon's habitat is extremely small, so they need every inch of it. There is nowhere else they can go. Humans, however, are rapidly taking over. Land for logging, farming, and for human living space has cut into the animals' territory. Tourism is also taking its toll. Other people **poach** the prey that dragons need to survive, such as deer. The illegal exotic animal trade takes dragons, too. Nature poses other threats in the form of tsunamis, earthquakes, volcanoes, and rising sea levels.

The International Union for Conservation of Nature (IUCN) is a worldwide organization that keeps watch on threatened species. Their "red list" shows dragons as endangered. They're in trouble, but not yet super seriously. In 2024, only about 3,400 Komodo dragons remained in the wild. But this is good news. In 2019, the count was fewer than 2,000.

A big reason for this success is the efforts at Komodo National Park, established in 1980. Its dedicated workers focus on preserving the dragons' habitat and prey. They also educate people and have put "anti-poaching" laws in place. They're making sure the local population understands and supports the work to protect their native reptile species. The nonprofit Komodo Survival Program (KSP) is another committed Indonesia-based organization.

Worldwide, other "save-the-dragon" efforts are ongoing, too. Nashville Zoo, which houses the largest Komodo dragon habitat in the Americas, works closely with KSP. Scientific studies are also revealing interesting new information. Some researchers are focusing on Komodo dragon genetics. Another study found that dragon teeth resemble those of the extinct theropod dinosaur. All these efforts matter. Everyone who pays attention to Komodo dragon survival is helping. It means these magnificent, ferocious creatures should not only survive. They will thrive.

FAMILY ALBUM

SNAPSHOTS

Westerners knew nothing about Komodo dragons until 1910. They were a species Europeans had never encountered before, which they first called "land crocodiles."

The largest Komodo dragon ever measured was 10.3 feet (3.1 m) long. It weighed 366 pounds (166 kg).

On the islands where they live, Komodo dragons are nearly the only carnivores, and the biggest. Their only real threat is other dragons.

Komodo dragons stalk animals much larger than themselves. But baby dragons make up about 10 percent of the adult dragon's diet.

Even a large, 198-pound (90-kg) deer doesn't have a chance against a smaller-size, 88-pound (40-kg) Komodo dragon.

Komodo dragons can consume up to 80 percent of their body weight at one time.

It takes Komodo dragons several weeks to digest a big meal. So they might eat as few as 12 meals a year.

Komodo dragons make few sounds. They do hiss, usually when feeding, mating, or under attack.

When preparing their nests, female dragons dig multiple holes to fool egg-eating animals. These holes can be as deep as 6.5 feet (2 m).

Instead of digging their own nests, female Komodo dragons often take over the abandoned ground nests of some birds.

Although it's rare, female Komodo dragons sometimes lay fertilized eggs without having mated. The babies that result are always male.

WORDS to Know

ambush to attack by surprise from a hidden place

apex predator an animal at the top of the food chain; an animal that hunts and is not usually hunted by other animals

carnivorous meat-eating

conservationist someone who works to protect and preserve animals and the environment

ectothermic cold-blooded, or unable to control one's own body temperature

extinct no longer in existence

hatchling an animal that has just recently broken out of its egg

instinctively resulting from an inborn or naturally occurring knowledge or understanding

poach illegally capture or kill animals for profit

species a group of living things that have shared characteristics and are able to reproduce with one another

LEARN MORE

Books

Fickett, Jamie. *Crazy Lizards*. Coral Springs, Fla.: Seahorse Publishing, 2025.

Roggio, Sarah. *Komodo Dragons vs. Wild Boars*. Minneapolis: Lerner Publications, 2025.

Weakland, Mark. *Komodo Dragons*. Mankato, Minn.: Black Rabbit Books, 2024.

Websites

"Komodo Dragon." Britannica Kids.
https://kids.britannica.com/kids/article/Komodo-dragon/390780.

"Komodo Dragon." Ducksters.
https://www.ducksters.com/animals/komodo_dragon.php

"Komodo Dragon." National Geographic Kids.
https://kids.nationalgeographic.com/animals/reptiles/facts/komodo-dragon.

Documentaries

Bergmann, Manuel, dir. *The World of Dragons*. Manuel Bergmann, 2020.

Cole, Chris, dir. *Komodo: Secrets of the Dragon*. BBC, 2011.

Lemire, Jean, dir. *The King of Lizards*. Documentary Central, 2023.

Note: Every effort has been made to ensure that any websites listed above were active at the time of publication. However, because of the nature of the Internet, it is impossible to guarantee that these sites will remain active indefinitely or that their contents will not be altered.

Visit

ABQ BIOPARK

Take an outdoor stroll with Komodo dragon Indah and her handler.

903 10th Street S.W.
Albuquerque, NM 87102

NASHVILLE ZOO

See Lil Sebastian, the zoo's largest Komodo dragon, in the largest Komodo exhibit in the Americas.

3777 Nolensville Pike
Nashville, TN 37211

KOMODO NATIONAL PARK

Get up close and personal with Komodo dragons in their natural island habitat.

East Nusa Tenggara
Indonesia

SMITHSONIAN'S NATIONAL ZOO

Meet male Komodo dragons Murphy and Onyx at the Reptile Discovery Center.

3001 Connecticut Avenue N.W.
Washington, D.C. 20008

INDEX